I0461334

Properly Prepared

Pugs Can Fly!

A Practically Painless Travel Guide and Priceless Points About Pugs

BY
ELIZABETH O'CARROLL

CELESTAR
Publishing

Properly Prepared
Pugs *Can* Fly!

A Practically Painless Travel Guide and Priceless Points About Pugs by Elizabeth O'Carroll

Published by Celestar Publishing LLC

30 N Gould St Ste R

Sheridan, WY. 82801

Copyright © 2022 Celestar Publishing LLC

All rights reserved. No portion of this book may be reproduced in any form without permission from the publisher, except as permitted by U.S. copyright law. For permissions contact: celestarpublishing@gmail.com

Edited by Latifah M. Salaudeen and Omer Hassan

Cover Illustration by Sharleen Rachel Sutjitra

Research and medical content contributions:

Dr. Tahira Mukhtar Certified Veterinarian

and Afsheen Mujutaba.

ISBN: 979-8-9861660-2-5 (print)

TABLE OF CONTENTS

CHAPTER 1: The Little Things About Little Pugs   06

CHAPTER 2: Pug facts that might surprise you   12

CHAPTER 3: The problem with pugs-

Brachycephalic Syndrome   20

CHAPTER 4: Can Pugs Fly?

Air Travel with a snub-nosed dog   24

CHAPTER 5: Tips for risk-free travel with your pug   32

CHAPTER 6: A few more tips to help with the journey   36

CHAPTER 7: Checklist to consider

before dog airline travel   38

CHAPTER 8: Pros and cons of traveling with pugs   46

CHAPTER 9: Travel options available   56

CHAPTER 10: The Final Word   64

Pug Tracker Worksheets   68

References: 89

Dedication

To all pug lovers globally, I trust there will be grand adventures ahead
for pug families and that this book provides some wisdom to ease
the planning process.

Special thanks to my research professionals; Dr. Tahira Mukhtar
Certified Veterinarian and Afsheen Mujutaba for their contributions
to this book.

Of course, to 'Ponyo" our family pug who has added
extreme joy and love to the chapters of our lives.

Foreword

Pugs are a unique breed that comes with the worthiness of understanding their background, physical, emotional, and overall needs. Whether you have a pug or you are welcoming a pug into your family; at some point you may find an opportunity or necessity of traveling.

Preparing a pug and your family for travel can best be coined with the age-old adage: "An ounce of prevention is worth a pound of cure." This guide was created out of the inspiration and need to travel with my own pug whose name is Ponyo. Ponyo will join us throughout the pages of this book and many of her 'distant relatives.'

Enjoy your travels with your pug and take a lot of pictures of your pug antics and irresistible personality traits!

The family pug, "Ponyo."

CHAPTER 1

The Little Things

About Little

Pugs

Owning a pet is a delight and when it comes to the selection, people can think of no other better pet than a dog. A particular breed of large popularity is the PUG. It's strange to know the unconditional love that pugs have gained over time. People's liking for them is just overwhelming. My first encounter with a pug was around eight years ago when my son wanted to surprise his girlfriend with a pug for Christmas. We made a trip to the pet market in search of a hand full of wrinkles. The compact stature and those lovable eyes were enough to get us hooked, and a funny little snort just nailed the decision of bringing the 'pug ball' home for the holidays.

Photo by Michelle Middleton on Unsplash

Pugs are amongst the oldest breeds and have been ancient companions since 400 BC.1 Many historians believe that they first originated in China.2 The Empress of China deemed pugs so essential that they had their servants build dog houses in the royal quarter and serve them the finest foods to dine on. Probably, not a bad life after all! Across cultures, pugs have taken on a strong association with royalty. They have been favorites even for the Royal British family because of their compact size and because they can fit in smaller spaces. For ages, dogs have been the epitome of loyalty, and pugs are no such exception. They have forever been able to warm the hearts and laps of their owners alike.

Photo by charles deluvio on Unsplash

From Chinese to Tibetan monks these pugs have always been an apple of society's eye. Their popularity has since then ranged from China to Japan and Russia and eventually to Europe. You no longer need to have a title to own a pug and today they have made a valuable place in posters and laptop desktops and are the most lovable household companion.

Most pugs have a round squishy face, a wrinkled forehead, a short nose, a stud body, stubby stature, and a curled tail. They have shorter legs as compared to a larger body. Pugs have wonderful temperaments and a slightly comical build. Their incredible sense of humor makes them commonly known as 'The Clown.' They are an intelligent, playful, and people-loving breed which is why they have such a lively atmosphere around them.

They are bred for companionship and proudly portray a very sedentary

lifestyle. I relate to a pug to a large extent. I would love to spend hours and hours forever on the sofa without doing anything with a companion who loves to do the same and makes me feel less guilty. There has been nothing more therapeutic for me than to come to a pug who starts encircling me and following me everywhere. It is difficult to ignore a pug after a stressful day at work. As soon as I am greeted at the door by Ponyo, I don't feel any stress once I am with my pug. Ponyo will wheeze, snort, and shake her toy around which makes me grin from ear to ear.

Pugs are crazy eaters and very fussy when it comes to food. They are so food driven that they can eat themselves to death. She can eat so frequently and so willingly even if she is fed six times a day. Because of this, your people food should be out of reach as they can eat technically anything at any time. I normally feed my pug homemade food in combination with store-bought food.

Ponyo's favorites are boiled chicken, egg, or raw carrots. For a treat, I offer her healthy dog biscuits or seedless fruits. She loves bananas!

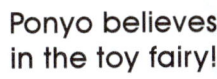

Ponyo believes in the toy fairy!

Pugs can sometimes be a difficult breed; people often have many questions about them. 'Are pugs safe to be around?' is a common one, nevertheless, there is nothing to worry about. Pugs are by far the safest breed of dogs, and if kids are not safe with pugs, they would not be with any dog on earth. They have a good relationship with elderly people because they are not very physically active and would prefer slow short strolls in the park over very rigorous runs, just like older folks do. This breed does not require much exercise and you should not exhaust them. They sleep for approximately 14 hours a night. Yes, you got that right, more than you do.

Instead of taking a run, pugs would much rather spend quality play time with you. Unlike other dogs, if you throw a frisbee or a disk and ask him to fetch it, you'd just have to stand there waiting, as your pug is very likely to hold it in its mouth and sit in some corner playing with it, or probably run away with it thinking you are the one who is supposed to chase it. Funny, isn't it? My pug is such a comedian, she would start barking in her sleep giving you the impression that someone is after her life, and at other times whine in excitement and I know she is dreaming about treats and is yearning for an extra one, or even being startled in her sleep by running after butterflies.

Photo by
Jorge
Zapata on
Unsplash

1 Giorgio, Katie Mills. "Pug"

2 Jennifer Wilber, "The History of Pugs in Ancient China," PetHelpful, April 13, 2022, https://pethelpful.com/dogs/This-History-of-Pugs-in-Ancient-China.

CHAPTER 2

Pug facts that
might surprise
you

Pug life is 'Thug life.' Those adorable 'spoiled packets of energy' have so much to their existence that you will be surprised.

1. A group of pugs is called a 'grumble.'

Imagine the name for such lovely creatures who are so full of energy and will follow you all the time, and everywhere. They are such attention-seekers and cannot tolerate the owner ignoring him in the least. They tend to follow you like a shadow. I remember mine waiting outside the loo waiting for me to come out. Insane, isn't it?

2. The origin of the peculiar face

That peculiar squishy smashed face of a pug that makes it look genuinely cute is due to a deformity in the skull. This deformity is hereditary and brings along risks of breathing issues and other related health problems.

3. Pugs are sleepy heads

Pugs are fond of sleeping. On average they spend around 14 hours a day sleeping, minus the time they spend snuggling and cozying on their favorite corners, and sofas which I guess is a major portion of their wake time

Photo by Priscilla Du Preez on Unsplash

Photo
by Martin May
on Unsplash

4. Tendency towards obesity

Pugs are very prone to gaining weight and have a stronger tendency towards obesity, and since they belong to the brachycephalic breed you might consider a mini workout routine with them that could keep them active. (Weight Tracker worksheet)

5. Pugs were bred to be lap dogs

Since their origin, pugs were meant to be lap dogs, owing to their small size and rounded stubby stature, people have found it quite easy to keep one as a pet. Pugs have very subtly snorted and panted their ways into the hearts of people. The Chinese purposefully created marks to have wrinkles on their forehead which resembled a Chinese mark that means 'Prince.' This is what explains their sassy attitude!

6. Pugs need to pee frequently

Pugs have small bladders; hence, you must be careful and take them out at least thrice a day to avoid any accidents taking place in the house. Small bodies mean compact organs, and the brachycephalic is no exception as problems are likely to arise a little too soon.

Ponyo taking a much-needed rest.

7. Two tail curls

The pug has a little tail with 2 curls, which curl up towards their bodies, and that is supposed to be a perfect tail.

8. Health effects

Health issues with pugs are their major downsides. The most common health issues are heart problems, encephalitis, or the inflammation of the brain, and sometimes eye problems too. Therefore, if you are planning to own a pug you must have a friend who is a vet, or your vet might eventually become a friend because of the frequent number of visits you need to take. Having top-notch medical insurance is also beneficial to ensure the pug has a quality and longer life and prompt treatment. A pug is a veterinarian's ideal patient as he is often looking

for medical assistance, also sometimes a nightmare as it is exceedingly difficult to revive a serious respiratory condition.

9. It's not easy to train pugs

Pugs are more like kids; they get bored very easily. I cannot yet decide who is tougher to train, a pug, or a toddler. Like other dogs, pugs are naughty, and a little rebellious too. They get distracted easily and hence require quite a surplus of tolerance and can be challenging work to train them. Consistency is key!

10. Pugs are not good athletes

When it comes to being physically fit, pugs are not the perfect sports material. It has this peculiar body structure and short stature with short legs that do not make them particularly good swimmers or runners. It is because of this small size they are fondly known as the 'toy breeds.' On average, they might be able to run around 3 to 5 miles an hour. (Weekly Logbook-Activities)

11. Pugs shed a ton of hair!

Unlike some dogs, Pugs do not have shedding seasons. It is because they shed hair all year round. You must have a heavy-duty vacuum cleaner to tackle and clean the constant collection of hair hiding around the house that is caused by the frequent shedding of hair.

12. Pugs cannot cool the air they breathe

A flat nose on pugs makes it difficult for them to regulate the air they breathe; as a result, they go through many complications such as an increased heart rate, panting, and sometimes even restlessness. Pugs are a perfect example of a breed that suffers from brachycephalic syndrome, more commonly known as brachycephalic airway obstruction syndrome. (BAOS).

13. Breathing problems

Their facial structure makes it difficult to take long and deep breaths, which is why you might hear a pug snuffling while running around. It is because of a short nose and smashed faces that obstruct the breathing pathways. Pugs are brachycephalic, meaning their noses are pushed in more than other dogs. This is probably also the reason they might not be the best swimmers and may have trouble on airplanes.

14. Pugs are clownish adorable furry friends

People who keep pugs as pets are well acquainted with their funny nature. Their snores are unbelievably loud, as loud as a lawnmower! They are incredibly noisy when they are asleep. Pugs are known for their peculiar snorts and farts, and the comical way they carry this trait. Ponyo becomes embarrassed after letting out an SBD (silent but deadly) fart and she will hide under the bed.

15. No one messes with a pug

Pugs are known for their loyalty, and to the extent that people relate to Napoleon's wife Josephine's pet pug named Fortuné. Josephine had a strong liking for her pug and the feelings were mutual. On the night of their marriage, Napoleon wanted Josephine to kick Fortune from the marriage bed. Fortune instead decided to bite Napoleon and teach him a lesson.

Photo by sarandy westfall on Unsplash

I can't say I blame Napoleon for not wanting Fortune in the same bed they shared. Ponyo has a way of sleeping all OVER the bed. Coupled with loud snores, there is not much sleep to be gained with a pug in your bed!

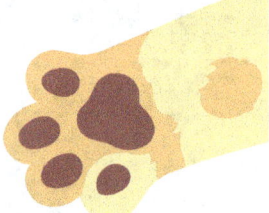

CHAPTER 3

The problem
with pugs- Brachycephalic

Syndrome

Photo by Mika
Baumeister on Unsplash

Every beautiful thing on earth comes with a price and the pug is no exception. There is more to their health than those "puggly-cute" looks that make them so adorable. Brachycephalic breeds of dogs are easily identified by their shortened snouts or faces that appear flat and, as a result, have narrow nostrils and smaller airways. Pugs are a classic example of a breed suffering from the brachycephalic syndrome. This condition has more to do with the anatomy and the

congenital deformity of the pug, rather than the pathology involved. A pug's skull is structured in such a way that it results in deformity which makes their nostrils and palate too small, hindering proper airflow and resulting in shortness of breath.

This explains the frequent snorting and panting noises they make. My first night with Ponyo was such a disaster. After a whole tiresome day when I settled in to retire for the night, the sleepy head pug snored out her night to glory. Snores are so loud that you probably cannot think of having a peaceful night's sleep if you aren't used to sounds around. Nevertheless, the pug is so adapted to this trait and is very content when he sees you amused at periodical snorts and wheezes along the way. Due to this condition, pugs tend to get exhausted even after a gentle exercise and start panting and rolling out their tongue to gasp for air. Summer days are terrible for pugs because they struggle to pant and can acquire heat stroke quickly.

At this point, you may be wondering, are there other problems that can be associated with brachycephalic syndrome? The answer is yes! The brachycephalic syndrome has been linked not only to the lungs, but also to problems related to the gastrointestinal tract including bronchial collapse, gastroesophageal reflux, and chronic gastritis. The good news is there is a way out. Brachycephalic syndrome is a genetic deformity that cannot be cured, however, there are specific surgical procedures that can help. A few of them are:

    1. Cutting back or resecting the soft palate to shorten it.

    2. Tonsillectomy- a procedure in which the tonsils are removed to give space to the narrowed passageway.

    3. Corrective operations to widen the nostrils opening up the way and making it easier to breathe.

Photo by James Tiono on Unsplash

CHAPTER 4

Can Pugs Fly?

Air Travel with a snub-nosed

dog

The brachycephalic breed is also commonly known as the 'snub-nosed breed.' People who keep pugs as pets are very aware that these furry balls are the most happening companions around BUT are a total contrast when it comes to traveling. Snub-nosed dogs are often at high risks when it comes to travel, particularly, air travel. Brachycephalies have a shorter muzzle and flat nose due to which they cannot breathe as efficiently as dogs with normal snouts. Because of this, they also have difficulty cooling off their bodies in stressful conditions such as playing and exercising—activities which heat their bodies.

If you are the proud owner of any of the brachycephalic breeds, such as a Pug, French Bulldog, or Boston Terrier, you should know that the move is not going to be that easy. Snub-nosed dogs have trouble breathing and difficult respiration under normal conditions, so imagine what agony they might go through when they are traveling by air. Air travel can worsen their respiratory problems and coupled with the higher altitudes; the cargo holds either heats up or becomes too cold.

Both scenarios are aversive for a pug.

Besides, there is no one to look after the pug in the cargo hold which means immediate help cannot be provided in critical circumstances. Situations such as these have been the cause of many deaths of snub-nosed dogs on flights, forcing the airlines to change their traveling policies keeping in consideration the hazards this poses to them

When a pet becomes a household member, one cannot abandon it. Temperamentally, pugs are so attached to the people around them, that they are attention-seeking and need your attention 24/7. They are so clingy that you cannot possibly think of relocating or moving around without them because of their sheer attachment.

Thankfully, there are many alternate options and management guidelines available that ensure safe and hassle-free travel for both you and your pet. Proper planning and precautionary measures have

25

made sure many brachycephalies are commuting risk-free, reducing the death toll rate on flights.

Pugs Traveling On Plane Some Data of Causalities

Dogs have been known to die when traveling through planes for many years. However, there has been no clear explanation as to why this occurs. Some theories suggest that dogs may be injured by the turbulence of the air or by the sharp edges of the aircraft seats. Some dog owners believe that their furry friends may become lost in the crowd and don't receive enough attention from airport security.

The Department of Transportation of the United States released a report on animal injury and death. The report covers all incidents that took place during the last few years. They report all the incidents, both with and without fatalities. The report also provides statistics on the incidents.

Photo by charlesdeluvio on Unsplash

From 2005 to 2010, there were more than 120 dog deaths reported and most of them were flying through cargo. Almost half of these dogs are flat-face dogs, which is a cause for concern because they are at risk of being crushed or killed in the crates that transport them. Most of these dogs involved Pugs, French bulldogs, and English bulldogs.

Many airlines have banned flat -face dog breeds from traveling through planes, reducing the number of deaths of these animals. This policy is important because it can help to prevent dog breeds from becoming a problem on planes, and it can also save lives. In 2017 there were only 24 deaths reported and only 3 of them are snub-face dogs.

The travel of animals by plane is a common occurrence and is often dangerous for the animals. There are more than 500,000 animals that travel by plane during this time. The number of fatalities caused is less when compared to the number of animals traveled but still necessary precautions must be taken.

What Travel Conditions Are Stressful For My Dog?

The health issues that flat-face dog breeds suffer from when traveling by plane are many and varied. Pugs that are commonly traveling through planes suffer from health issues such as respiratory problems. Aside from that issue, there are many other chronic conditions like obesity and diabetes that are very dangerous for your pup.

Photo by
Benjamin
Wong on
Unsplash

Flat-faced dog breeds can suffer from many health issues when traveling on planes. Some of these issues include breathing problems, heart problems, and epilepsy. It is important to be aware of the health risks before traveling with a pug and make sure to take necessary precautions.

Advance Age

Pugs traveling with humans are always at risk of getting sick. It is important to take regular precautions to avoid sickness in these fur balls and ensure that they are well-prepared for the trip. Advanced age can affect a Pug's susceptibility to illness, so it is important to have accurate information on when a dog is ready for travel.

One of the most serious medical conditions that can affect senior pugs are age-related arthritis and organ failure. Additionally, an older Pug may be more susceptible to injuries while traveling.

Obesity

Some dogs may be more prone to developing health issues when traveling because of the various environmental factors that can affect their everyday lives. Obesity is a common problem in all dogs and can lead to heart problems, joint problems, and other issues. Some vets say that obesity may even increase the risk of some types of cancer. So, before you take your brachiocephalic pup on his next long trip, make sure he's weighed and had his routine check-up.

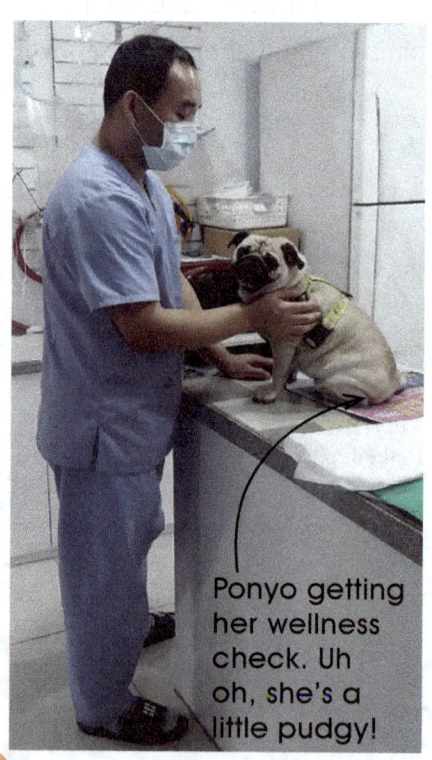

Ponyo getting her wellness check. Uh oh, she's a little pudgy!

Ponyo getting her wellness check. Uh oh, she's a little pudgy!

Humidity and heat

Dogs traveling through hot and humid countries are at a higher risk for respiratory problems, as well as other health conditions. These problems can be significant enough to require medical attention, and sometimes even lead to death. In addition, the contagious nature of some dog diseases can make traveling through these areas an especially risky proposition.

Dogs that travel through planes may get a temperature-controlled environment inside the plane. Before that, they are loaded last and off-loaded first. This makes them susceptible to heat and humidity. Dogs that travel through planes are often difficult to keep cool because of their enthusiastic behavior and constant body motion.

Photo by Bruce Galpin on Unsplash

Dogs are not allowed to travel on Airline itineraries if the ambient temperature is more than 85 degrees Fahrenheit. This rule applies to the entire itinerary from departure, stops, and destination. If you have a flat-face dog breed, the condition becomes worse. The extra heat and humidity can cause the breathing issues to become worse. So, it is recommended not to travel with your Pug if the ambient temperature is above 75 degrees Fahrenheit.

What Are The Things You Should Be Aware Of Before Travelling?

While it may not be necessary, some people believe that sedating your dog before traveling will help them feel more relaxed and less anxious. Some dogs may also benefit from being sedated to reduce their stress levels on the plane. It can also help to reduce the risk of anxiety and other behaviors during the trip. This can also make the trip more comfortable for both the dog and the traveler. In the case of snubbed-face dogs never use any kind of sedatives because there are some risks associated with doing so. One is that the medication can make the dog sleepy and unsteady on its feet while on the plane. Additionally, it can make the dog more liable to get sick if it takes in traveling air. It also makes their breathing rate slow and lowers their blood pressure. In case of an overdose, it affects your dog's cognition skills, making them more confused and not able to understand what's going on around them.

Sedation can put your brachycephalic dog in more danger rather than helping him. Most Airlines have implemented a rule to not let any dog on board if sedated.

Photo by sarandy westfall on Unsplash

CHAPTER 5

Tips for risk-free

travel with your

Pug

Traveling with animals should be backed up with proper care and appropriate measures. Brachycephalic are a breed susceptible to altitude changes and need a little more extra planning and special precautions to ensure a trouble-free, happy flying experience. Since it is not always feasible to travel by road, here's how you can make traveling a pleasant experience for both you and your pug:

1. Opt for a pet-friendly airline

Choose an airline that allows pet travel, specifically brachycephalic. Many pet-friendly airlines oblige and facilitate the movement of pugs, and they have special arrangements made in this regard. They double-check if the cargo hold temperature is controlled and the water supplies are assessed before and after flying. You should check if the airline has specific rules and regulations to have a pug on board. Read the document thoroughly before you embark on your journey. It is better to be safe than sorry!

2. Consult your vet

If your pug has had regular appointments with the vet, it would be nice to talk to him about your traveling and get your pet checked before the flight to prevent any mishaps or troubles that might otherwise arise due to its health condition. Being a pet parent is not easy, and it is always good to seek professional assistance to be on the safe side.

3. Make sure your pet is healthy

Pugs tend towards obesity. Even under normal circumstances, obesity in brachycephalic breeds tends to create problems in their movement. Overweight pugs are at greater risk when flying. If they are stressed or overheated, it could cut off the air supply and obstruct breathing. Fit and healthy pets lower these risk factors and travel problem-free.

4. Select a suitable crate

Small-sized brachycephalic breeds can travel in the flight. Nevertheless, they will need to be placed in a crate, which is according to their size. An ideal container should be slightly larger than its size to give enough room for air circulation and a little movement to the pug. The extra space provides more air supply that helps dogs with breathing problems.

Photo by charlesdeluvio on Unsplash

5. Get your dog used to the flight crate.

Acclimating your pug to their crate that you will carry in flight is always an ingenious idea. This will save your pet from panicking and will not consider it an alien object. Accommodating your pet to a new crate and training him before they fly will link it with positive memories and prevent it from creating problems on the flight. It will also reduce their stress level and provide them comfort during the flight. (Flight crate checklist)

6. Hydrate your pug thoroughly

Before you embark on your journey, ensure your pet is thoroughly hydrated. This should be checked days before the travel to avoid any dehydration that might occur at altitudes. This will help their bodies

to cool down as it is difficult for brachycephalic pets to manage in warm conditions. You should also attach a water bottle to the crate or keep a travel water bowl for your pet to drink from during the flight.

7. Carry along your dog's vaccination and health records

Make sure you carry your dog's vaccination records and other data so you can produce them to the authorities once required. Even people around you or in the aircraft might want to feel safe when there is an animal on board. (Vaccination checklist)

8. Restrict food in advance

Feed your pug a balanced diet and restrict heavy food at least 12 hours before the flight. Doing so will prevent nausea at heights or poop, which is uncontrollable with a full belly. You would not want the passengers to feel sick due to the toxic odor in the air-conditioned aircraft. Make the travel experience pleasant for both you and the passengers too.

(Food Tracker Worksheet)

Ponyo eating her one meal per day at the Pet Hotel.

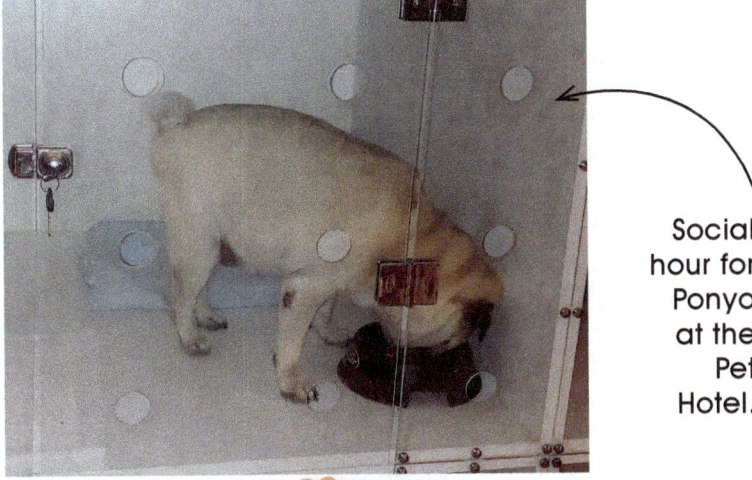

Social hour for Ponyo at the Pet Hotel.

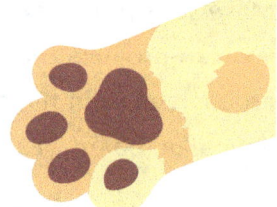

CHAPTER 6

A few more tips

to help with the

Journey

Besides considering the foundational instructions on travel with pugs, here are a few more general guidelines that can assist you and help you travel easily with your pug on an airplane. (Pugs Packing List Worksheet)

- Open the air vent above your seat to enable a smooth flow of air in the direction of your pug's snout.

- A pet carrier with zipping sides, can help the pug poke out his head if he wants to. The open zip allows them to breathe easily compared to having it zippered shut.

- Tire your pug out with physical activities or ample play time before the flight so that the dog can take the time on the plane to rest and probably take a much-needed nap. Remember, do not overexert the pug as they are sensitive dogs, and stressed-out pugs are likely to find traveling very troublesome.

- You could carry zip lock bags and fill them with ice before travel or ask the flight attendant to do so that the pug can use it to cool himself off. There are also Cooling Gel mats made for dogs that you can put at the bottom of their carrier.

- Keep a check and know the placements of the oxygen mask in an air flight in case you might have any emergency arise during the travel.

- Avoid using thick heavy blankets and clothing items in the pet carrier or on the pug, as they tend to heat up quickly and takes a lot of time to cool down their body temperature.

CHAPTER 7

checklist to consider

before dog

Air line

Travel

Weighing down the pros and cons is inevitable when it comes to anything, but before you plan a journey with your snub -nosed friend, you would like to glance at a little checklist so that you are mentally convinced that your pug is ready to travel. Check this out:

Assess the pug's overall health

It is established that pugs have sensitive health issues. They are amongst the most vulnerable breeds of dogs, even under normal conditions. When you intend to relocate or travel with your pug, it's best to schedule a visit to the vet to assess any breathing or underlying cardiac issues that might be aggravated during travel.

Documents

Many travelers take note of the required documents before travelling with their pets, but sometimes forget to include important papers such as a pet passport or animal welfare certificate. Here are simple documents to remember before traveling with your furry friend: (Pet Trackers Worksheets!)

- **A valid passport for your dog.**

- **A first-class ticket for your pet.**

- **Your pet's animal welfare certificate.**

- **Health and safety information for your pet.**

- **An animal boarding or quarantine station list.**

- **Pet insurance certificate.**

- **Recent vaccination certificates.**

- **Travel insurance policy for your dog.**

Check if your pug has the temperament to fly.

Like human beings, not all animals have the same temperament. Pugs are the most social and people-loving breed, yet they might not accept the environmental changes during travel, especially with air travel. Air travel can prove to be scary for a pug since it has to undergo high altitudes and sometimes weird sounds that we hear in an aircraft. It might also refuse to be alone in the cargo vault.

Will your pet enjoy the journey?

As I previously mentioned, not all pugs would like to leave their stable environment and enjoying themselves with their people. Though for pugs the presence of his known people is therapeutic, so are his cozy corners and the sofa. Considering the pug's sedentary lifestyle, it is highly likely for him not to be ecstatic with the new environment or surroundings. Even if it is a five-star pug palace.

Check for pet-friendly hotels.

Before you embark on your journey, it is always wise to list pet-friendly hotels that cater to dogs. It is always tiresome to make decisions on the spot and hunt down prospective places to stay with limited time available. We are all aware of the stress that unfamiliar cities can be when you are not familiar with hotels. This anxiety has a trickle-down effect to your pug. They are highly sensitive and tuned in to their people. (Dog Friendly Hotel & Socialization Worksheet)

Ponyo at the pet hotel
Doggy Day Camp!

You would also like to check on the following things to see if your pug is travel-ready

- **He is okay with strangers or other dogs around**

- **He does not mind socializing with unknown faces**

- **He is used to the carrier and would not panic if he must spend time in it**

- **He is accustomed to unfamiliar places, environments, and spaces**

- **Does not get nervous very easily**

- **Does not suffer from anxiety**

- **Can manage without the owner's attention for random periods**

- **Is not obese and is of a healthy weight**

Social hour for Ponyo at the Pet Hotel.

Watch out for these signs that your pug is not travel-ready

- They are obese and find it challenging to move around efficiently

- They suffer from height fright or claustrophobia

- Suffer from anxiety and nervousness

- Do not get along well with new people or other dogs and take time settling down

- They are used to their home environment and spaces and cannot give them up

- Are they on medications for breathing issues or other underlying problems?

Gather All the Supplies

If you are traveling with your Pug, it is important to gather necessary pet supplies before traveling. This includes food, water, toys, and other comfort items. By knowing what items you will need and storing them in a safe place, you can ensure that your pet is taken care of while on the go. Here are some of the important supplies to gather. (Pug Packing List Worksheet).

Photo by Darinka
Kievskaya on Unsplash

Toys

Dogs love to play and explore, but sometimes they get lost in the shuffle during travel. A good way to keep your dog entertained is to bring along a toy for them to play with. Not only will this give your dog some mental stimulation, but it can also help you avoid any potential accidents or injuries.

Food and Water Containers

When traveling with a Pug, it is important to keep their food and water containers along. This will help to ensure that they have access to the food and water they need when necessary and that no accidents happen.

Dog Waste Bags

Pet waste is a big problem when traveling. It can smell bad, make your luggage smell bad, and create a mess. It's important to keep your pet waste bags along when traveling so you can avoid any problems.

Backpacks

Pugs are often seen traveling with their owners, but it's important to keep your dog's backpack along when traveling. This is because whether you are traveling via plane or the car your Pugs need treats, water, and food and you have to keep them in their backpack to access them easily.

Food

Most Pugs love to eat their favorite food, so it's important to have their dog's favorite food with them when traveling. This is because not all states have the same dog food available that your dog likes. It's important to keep an extra food bag in case of any emergency.

Dog Bed

Keeping your Pug's bed with you on the go will make your trip much easier and more comfortable for both you and your pet. Not only will your Furry friend have a comfortable place to sleep, but he will feel more comfortable when he has a familiar thing around.

First Aid Kit

Traveling with a Pug can be a lot of fun, but it can also be dangerous. One of the things you need to consider is if you have a first aid kit with you when traveling with your furry friend. A first aid kit can help you save yourself time and money in case something happens.

Photo by Diana Parkhouse on Unsplash

CHAPTER 8

Pros and cons
of traveling with
Pugs

Pet travel is on the rise these days, and it is a lovely feeling that you can take your pug with you like the rest of your family members. However, it isn't as easy as it sounds, and traveling with pets, especially pugs, is no picnic if you are not prepared. Besides thinking about the costs incurred, travel can also be stressful for certain dogs, and pugs top the list. As much as you would love your furry snub-nosed dog to accompany you to beautiful destinations, you also must consider certain things. Although people have formulated the best ways to ensure safe travel for their dogs, there are pros and cons that cannot be ignored. Here they are:

PROS

Guilt-free travel

People who own dogs, especially pugs, know their importance in their lives. Pugs are so lively and happy in their home atmosphere that one cannot possibly think of leaving them and going elsewhere. Traveling with your pug means you are moving around guilt-free and not missing them. It makes your time out full of contentment and joy, knowing that your furry friend is your companion and is enjoying and having the best time of their life. The sense of togetherness keeps you going and motivated as you know your pet very well and keeping him away with uncertainty about how he would be adjusting is just adding to the anxiety.

They provide great company.

Dogs are the best company in any place. They never let you feel lonely and are willing to follow you everywhere. You travel and discover new destinations together. Typically, a dog will enjoy novel places, be it sea sides, beaches or parks, or mountain hikes. They are your best consorts in a new place where you do not know anyone. They have a happy waggy-tongued expression all the time, which shows you how much they are enjoying themselves. Not to mention, all the

uncountable beautiful selfies you take together, creating memories for the album. You also get so much attention from people, especially kids as they absolutely adore seeing a pug.

Photo by Marcus Cramer on Unsplash

You will meet new people and socialize

Because pugs are so cute and fun-loving around children and older people alike, you will have new friends in no time. Pugs tend to explore the local neighborhood way too soon and, in return, will bring on many friends for socializing. Research shows that 60% of people who own pets are more likely to be social and gain more friends than those without pets. People from the local neighborhood are willing to offer help and guidance since they are now friends with your pug. Your dog might likely get a dog friend, too. Dogs have the disposition to stay young with little ones, but why only the young ones? The older people join the bandwagon of playing around with dogs. In short, the whole neighborhood is full of fun, laughs, and smiles.

Traveling with dogs slows down the hustle and bustle

When planning trips and excursions, we jot down so many destinations to see, hotels and sightseeing. So much to do in such little time that we often forget the true essence of holidays. Vacations are meant to calm and ease down the pace and the tiring schedules and take an edge off routine life. Dogs, in particular, help slow down your fast-paced plans as they provide much more enjoyment than just sightseeing. With your pug, you will have more slumbering around, cuddles, and cozying that add value to your time altogether.

Photo by Sneaky Elbow on Unsplash

Expands your horizon

Traveling with pugs enables you to venture and discover places and areas that are unseen and unplanned. When chalking out visiting destinations, we overlook the few not-so-famous places your dog will help you find out. The dog's temperament of wandering brings you to a site that is worth exploring and enjoying all the same, making beautiful memories with your furry ball. You might also explore destinations, sea views, and attractions that you might not have seen if it had not been for your pug ball. You also have ample time appreciating nature, which offers a soothing effect and helps unwind off the stress load we carry all day.

Save money on transportation.

If you own a small dog or a pug, it is a plus point as travel with smaller dogs is usually free, in many parts of the world. Small dogs can ride on public transit for free, which saves on the additional cost. Besides, there are many places in which reaching by car is not possible. These are the places where you can travel, thanks to your pug, and eventually, save on a few bucks that would go into transportation. Not only this, but you will also explore many places and spend more time there owing to the rest time you need to give your pug. Nature's bounty is absorbed in its best!

Ponyo with her favorite 'pug' pillow.

A sense of responsibility

Like humans, animals also have special needs, even more, when traveling. You groom and develop better as a person when looking after the needs of a pet. It creates a sense of empathy and responsibility as you show ownership to your pug and take care of its needs

and comfort even when he is away from home. The feelings are reversed when it comes to the pug. A pug showers you with so much affection, it vows to be with you through thick and thin, life and death. As history recalls, your dog is the most loyal of friends who will protect you in a new place amongst strangers.

Feel Like Home Outside of Your Home

There are many different ways to travel with your Pug, and the best way for you and your pup to feel at home is by taking the time to mix and match your travel habits. Whether you're traveling with a single dog or multiple dogs, certain things make traveling feel like home. First of all, you feel safe and have peace of mind that your favorite furry pal is along with you to protect you. Secondly, if you feel alone during the night and need cuddles your fur-ball can give you the best cuddles. He will also be alert if there is any danger around.

Photo by Igor Flek on Unsplash

CONS

Traveling with a pug can be expensive

Being affectionate with your pug is one story; incurring travel expenses is another. It is not at all easy making travel plans with your pet. And it is not only the travel cost that falls into account; there are accommodation costs too. Calculating both the travel and accommodation costs would bring the amount to a figure in which one more human being could travel. In short, to carry your pug with you, you must have a big heart and a bigger pocket.

Travel is stressful for pugs

Like humans, traveling is stressful for pugs, too. The ratio is much higher in the latter. Pugs suffer from anxiety during flight, and you can do nothing about it. Some airlines do not allow pets in the passenger area, which leaves no option for them except the cargo, which again creates panic for the pug. Sedation is an option that you technically cannot afford with any dog, specifically pugs. As a result, they suffer from breathing issues that might be aggravated due to sedation. Travel and new environments are also hectic for the pug, and it might take him a lot of time to settle down in the new place.

Not all hotels are pet friendly.

You need to do a lot of research when you leave home as not all hotels are pet friendly. They might allow access to the pet on the property in a kennel arrangement and not allow your pug to stay in the accommodation with his people. This could prove to be traumatic for your pug to stay away from you. For example, if you are planning a hitchhiking excursion, you might keep a makeshift tent with you in case the nearby hotel does not permit the accommodation of dogs. Personally, I like the idea of renting a van or a Recreational Vehicle for planned road trip excursions.

They can interrupt your travel plans.

Like I said, not every place you intend to visit will allow pets. Parks, beaches, and mountains are the most intriguing spots you would like to see. Then again, protected trails employ authorities to enforce the "No Dogs Allowed" dreaded rule. This can ruin your travel plan as you would have to either make it without your pet or cancel the visit altogether.

Photo by FLOUFFY on Unsplash

Extra luggage and packing

With an extra member on board, you would obviously require additional space for your pug's accessories. They might be bare necessities for the pug such as a collar, leash, food, and other necessary items such as toys, blankets, towels, waste bags, medication, and probably grooming items as well. (Travel Checklist)

No access to public transport

Carrying dogs with you might make you walk an extra mile. Some public transport does not allow pets on board, forcing you to take an expensive alternative for travel to a particular place or walk with your furry friend.

Pee time is trouble time.

Photo by Big Dodzy on Unsplash

Since pugs have little bladders, they need to pee quite often. You must time out your visit to places such as museums or any historical site as they do not facilitate a relief area for pets. Hence the program layout should be made in such a manner that it provides time back for a walk and your pug can relieve himself.

Market places or crowded areas are harder with a pug.

Though pugs are incredibly social animals, they react adversely to unfamiliar faces around crowded areas. Some people fear dogs, which creates a mess in overcrowded places. Women and kids screaming their hearts out of fear of the pug creates such havoc. In such a case, you will have to leave behind your pug in the hotel to avoid a mini circus.

Eating out is not always fun with a pug.

Dogs are not welcome everywhere. Certain lavish fine dining restaurants do not allow dogs around the dining area. There are some bakeries and grocery stores too, that are not dog-friendly because of their small spaces. Galleries, museums, and historical places also might not allow the entry of dogs, however trained, and civilized it is. So, when planning for the trip, ensure your itinerary supports the places and destinations that are dog friendly.

Photo by Albany Capture on Unsplash

CHAPTER 9
Travel options
Available

Ideally, several travel options are available for pugs. You could choose what suits you best looking into your pug's travel cost, time duration, and feasibility. Pugs require a lot of careful handling and planning when it comes to travel, and you would like to skim through all the available options before you decide your mode of travel. This also depends on how far the destination is. You can make your pick by considering the best travel options available. Here is a list of risk-free travel options which you can consider.

Photo by Mink
Mingle on
Unsplash

1. Traveling by air

Air travel is most stressful for any pet, especially a pug, merely due to its breathing issues when it reaches altitudes. Also, if it is not allowed entry in the cabin, he might have to be placed in the cargo cabin, with nasty sounds and lights, not to forget the movement of the luggage during the flight, which might harm the dog. If air travel is the only option

Photo by Casey Horner on Unsplash

available, see that your dog can travel with you in the passenger cabin, as traveling in the cargo cabin is monotonous for the pug. A list of precautions does minimize air travel risk, as sometimes, owing to the long distances, it is impractical to opt for any other mode of travel besides airplanes. In addition, upon entering a new state or country, there may be quarantine regulations. Be sure to have your pet's vaccination records with your travel documents. Some areas will require your pet to stay overnight or be health inspected before entering the outside atmosphere.

If you are considering international air travel, check with the country's embassy. For instance, the United States does not allow dogs to come into the country. They will be detained and sent back to the place of origin at the owner's expense. Domestic travel from state to state is more receptive yet do your homework and research your destination regulations! (Plane Tracker Worksheet)

2. Travel by train

Train travel is a convenient mode of travel for shorter distances. However, you do need to carry all the necessary documents and follow the same guidelines with your pet for safer easy-going travel. Even on trains, you must bring your pug in a carrier or leash it, as you would not like the other passengers to get disturbed. Also, trains allow only a specific limit of around twenty-five pounds or less to travel in compartments; otherwise, your pug will have to travel in the cargo compartment. You should also check the options available to facilitate your pug with pee and poop sessions. (Train Tracker Worksheet)

3. Traveling by car

Car travel is easy and fun-loving for both you and your pug. You travel at your own pace. However, general travel guidelines should also be implemented for safer, leisurely travel. You should plan stopover points. The dog should always be seated, strapped, and secured at the back to prevent the driver from being distracted. Also, allow only a little space on the window to prevent your pug from sticking out his head during travel. Car travel is the most recommended mode of travel as your pug is less likely to suffer travel sickness. Also, many stopovers for food, rest, and washrooms prevent travel stress with your pet. However, car travel is possible only to limited or nearby places. In long-distance areas, where cars cannot possibly commute, there is no other choice besides air travel.

Photo by Priscilla Du Preez

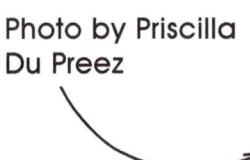

4. Traveling by boat, cruise ship or ferry

Boats, cruise ships and ferries are another route to consider. All forms of transportation will take ample preparation to get the trip in forward motion. For any type of sea travel, you will need to decide the route to port. Limited cruise lines will accept dogs for extended trips that require overnight or nights, such as America to Europe. Again, on a cruise ship the stabilization will be less turbulent for a pug, however, there might be a possibility that your pug will have to stay in the cargo containment area and monitored. Not to mention, super expensive and traumatic for a pug. In addition to all the standard paperwork, do your homework on your destination for entrance into the country requirements for your pug.

On the other hand, if you are just out for a day on the lake, prepare as you would for a two-year-old toddler. Have a life preserver vest, leash, and a towel that can be designated as their 'spot' to land when

Photo by Subin Saji on Unsplash

things get choppy. Pugs can suffer from overstimulation and have 'reverse hiccups' which sound a bit like they are choking. Calm your pug with a massage or tummy rub, and the hiccups will pass. Allow for 'shore breaks' where your pug can take care of business if you plan to be out all day. Monitor your pug's whereabouts if they get curious and wander off. Keep them hydrated and out of the direct sun to prevent them from overheating.

Finally, as with all water travel have a "Pug overboard" plan. Dogs get excited and want to jump without the logic of what comes next. (Ship/Cruise Tracker Worksheet)

FAQs

How Can I Carry A Pug On The Plane?

Pug travelling can be a fun, enlightening experience, especially if you have some prior knowledge of the destination and the requirements for flying. However, there are often specific guidelines that are available to accommodate those who want to fly with their pup. In general, most airlines allowed the Pugs to travel in the cabin along with you.

Some airlines only allowed dogs to travel in the cargo.

Is It Safe For Pugs To Travel In The Cargo?

The brachycephalic dog breed, like Pugs, may have difficulty maintaining a temperature balance when travelling in cargo areas. This can cause problems such as breathing difficulties and heatstroke. If the cargo areas have no temperature control, it may be unsafe for them to travel in cargo areas. The best way to avoid these problems is to always select an airline that has a controlled temperature and a better air circulation system.

Photo by Matthew Henry on Unsplash

Should I Tranquilize My Pug For A Long Flight?

Unfortunately, airline travel can be stressful for them, particularly when their owners are away. Some vets recommend that dogs should be tranquilized before departure to help reduce stress and make the trip more comfortable for all involved. However, in the case of flat-face dog breeds sedation is not recommended as it will decrease their blood pressure and cause breathing issues.

How To Choose An Appropriate Flight For My Pug?

Dog owners of all levels of experience and travel should consider the different types of flights available to them when choosing a flight for their furry friend. There are many factors to consider, including the airline, the time of year, and the destination.

Here are five simple tips to help you choose the best flight for your pug:

1. Research the airline before traveling.

2. Make a reservation for your Pug and yourself at the same time.

3. Don't book a flight in the busy seasons.

4. Always book a non-stop flight.

5. Always reconfirm your reservation a day before flying.

How to Select a Proper Crate for Your Air Travel?

It's best to select a crate that is approved by the airline and make sure that your Pug will get used to this crate before traveling. All the approved crates have the following basic features:

1. Crates should be large enough that your pup can easily move in them.

2. The crate must be leak proof.

3. There must not be any sharp corners or objects in the crate.

4. The crate must be properly ventilated.

5. The crate is clearly labeled with all your information.

Photo by Vidar Nordli-Mathisen on Unsplash

CHAPTER 10

The Final Word

Ponyo with Mike
and Summer (my
son and his wife)

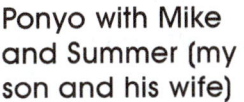

Even though traveling with a pug is no easy feat, pug owners know what their pug means to them. They are so used to their clowning around and funny gestures that they will miss them every moment of their journey. Dog owners consider pugs part of their family, and there is no way they would want to leave them behind. So, for all who are thinking of taking their pugs along, DO IT! Yes, it is difficult, yet what on earth isn't? If your pug meets the healthy travel check list and all the medical records line up, then why not? Where there is a will, there is always a way!

Trust me, the pain you go through will be so rewarding and heartwarming. And when you reflect on the good times, it will undoubtedly outweigh the problems you encountered. A little planning and research and you are good to go. Those smiling selfies and whoofs will always remind you of the lovely time you had together.

For Ponyo and I, after researching and writing this book, I have decided that it will have to be domestic travel by car or a van. We can camp out overnight or nap in the vehicle if we need to. Ponyo is an older pug, and she is a little obese. (don't tell her that) I won't risk her health or chance stressing her emotional sensitivity. I will pack her favorite stuffed animal, blanket, and her carrier that she knows is only HERS! I am older too, and our slow pace will be perfect for short strolls and a nap on the beach.

Happy and safe travels to you and your pug!

With my son Mike
and a baby Ponyo!

NOTE FROM THE AUTHOR

Thank you so much for spending time to read my book.

I would truly appreciate it if you could:

Review this: Reviews, even very brief ones are supportive to authors.

If you enjoyed the content and it was valuable, please consider leaving a review on Amazon or elsewhere as applicable.

Share this: When you share this book on social media, you're letting more people discover this story and word-of-mouth is the best marketing for any budding author!

If you would like copies of the Pug Worksheet Trackers in the back of this book, please send an e-mail to my Publishers at:

Celestarpublishing@gmail.com

They'll be happy to send you a PDF for your very own to print out and use for several travels in your future!

Thanks again and joyful journeys with your pug!

Oh, by the way...Ponyo is testing out teleportation and time machines, More updates on that in the future!

Pug

Tracker

Worksheets

PET INFORMATION

PET PHOTO

NAME	
BREED	
GENDER	
COLOR	
MICROCHIP	
BREED REGISTRATION	
BLOOD TYPE	
ALLERGIES	
COAT COLOR	
EYE COLOR	
SPECIAL MARKINGS	
MEDICAL CONDITIONS	
FAVORITE TOYS	
OTHER	

PET OWNER INFORMATION

PET OWNER PHOTO

NAME	
SURNAME	
ADDRESS	
POSTCODE	
CITY	
COUNTRY	
TELL NO.	
MAIL	

PET CLINIC INFORMATION

HOSPITAL NAME	
ADDRESS	
MAIL	
PHONE	

VETERINARIAN INFORMATION

HOSPITAL NAME	
ADDRESS	
MAIL	
PHONE	

IMMUNIZATION RECORDS

DATE	AGE	TYPE	GIVEN BY	NEXT DUE

PHOTO GALLERY

PET PHOTO

PET PHOTO

DATE:

DATE:

PET PHOTO

PET PHOTO

DATE:

DATE:

PET PHOTO

PET PHOTO

DATE:

DATE:

SOCIALIZATION LIST

PET NAME: _____

PEOPLE

PLACES

OTHER ANIMALS

OBJECTS

FOOD TRACKER

CITY: _____

BRAND	WHERE TO BUY	COST	NOTES

PETS GROOMING LOCATIONS
CITY: _____

Name:
Address:
Email:
Phone:
Price:
Payment Option:
Note:

Name:
Address:
Email:
Phone:
Price:
Payment Option:
Note:

Name:
Address:
Email:
Phone:
Price:
Payment Option:
Note:

Name:
Address:
Email:
Phone:
Price:
Payment Option:
Note:

Name:
Address:
Email:
Phone:
Price:
Payment Option:
Note:

Name:
Address:
Email:
Phone:
Price:
Payment Option:
Note:

DOG FRIENDLY LOCATIONS

NAME	ADDRESS	ADVANTAGES

ALLERGIES TRACKER

DATE DISCOVERED	ALLERGY	TREATMENT

FEED SCHEDULE

DAY	AM	PM
MONDAY		
TUESDAY		
WEDNESDAY		
THURSDAY		
FRIDAY		
SATURDAY		
SUNDAY		

DOG VACCINATION TRACKER

Age	Recommended (Core) Vaccinations	Optional Vaccinations	Date	Vaccinations Given
6 - 8 weeks	Distemper, parainfluenza	Bordetella		
10 - 12 weeks	DHPP [vaccinestor distemper, adenovirus (hepatitis), parainfluenza and parvovirus]	Coronavirus, Leptospirosis, Bordetella, Lyme disease		
12 - 24 weeks	Rabies	None		
14 - 16 weeks	DHPP	Coronavirus, Leptospirosis, Lyme disease		
12 - 16 months	Rabies, DHPP	Coronavirus, Leptospirosis, Bordetella, Lyme disease		
Every 1 - 2 years	DHPP	Coronavirus, Leptospirosis, Bordetella, Lyme disease		
Every 1 - 3 years	Rabies			

Notes: ....
....
....

PETS ER

Emergency Locations For Our Trip

CITY:	DATE:

Business Name:
Phone: **Email:**
Address:
Review Ratings:
Notes:

Business Name:
Phone: **Email:**
Address:
Review Ratings:
Notes:

Business Name:
Phone: **Email:**
Address:
Review Ratings:
Notes:

Business Name:
Phone: **Email:**
Address:
Review Ratings:
Notes:

WEEKLY CHECKLIST

WEEK: _____

MONDAY

🐾 FOOD	🐾 WALK	🐾 SOCIALIZATION
🐾 WATER	🐾 PLAY	🐾 MEDICATIONS

TUESDAY

🐾 FOOD	🐾 WALK	🐾 SOCIALIZATION
🐾 WATER	🐾 PLAY	🐾 MEDICATIONS

WEDNESDAY

🐾 FOOD	🐾 WALK	🐾 SOCIALIZATION
🐾 WATER	🐾 PLAY	🐾 MEDICATIONS

THURSDAY

🐾 FOOD	🐾 WALK	🐾 SOCIALIZATION
🐾 WATER	🐾 PLAY	🐾 MEDICATIONS

FRIDAY

🐾 FOOD	🐾 WALK	🐾 SOCIALIZATION
🐾 WATER	🐾 PLAY	🐾 MEDICATIONS

SATURDAY

🐾 FOOD	🐾 WALK	🐾 SOCIALIZATION
🐾 WATER	🐾 PLAY	🐾 MEDICATIONS

SUNDAY

🐾 FOOD	🐾 WALK	🐾 SOCIALIZATION
🐾 WATER	🐾 PLAY	🐾 MEDICATIONS

WEIGHT TRACKER

PET NAME: _____

DATE	WEIGHT	NOTES/ACTIONS

WEEKLY LOGBOOK

LOCATION:			WEEK:				

PET SCHEDULE OF ACTIVITIES	M	T	W	T	F	S	S

PUGS PACKING LIST
What to bring on our trip!

Checklist	Checklist
Health certificate and medical records	
Pet Passport	
Comb, brush, flea control products	
Pet wipes	
Paper towels and stain remover	
Dog food and treats	
Plenty of bottled water	
Food and water dishes	
Leash and poop bags	
Toy and blanket	

SHIP/CRUISE TRACKER

Pets Friendly Ship/Cruise

Destination: _____ **Number of Days:** _____

Travel Dates: _____ **Number of Nights:** _____

DEPARTURE

Leaving: _____ At: _____
Arriving: _____ At: _____
By: _____
Layovers: _____
Reference No.: _____

ARRIVAL

Leaving: _____ At: _____
Arriving: _____ At: _____
By: _____
Layovers: _____
Reference No.: _____

TRANSPORTATION

Ship/Cruise: _____
Pick Up: _____ Drop Off: _____
Company: _____
Contact: _____
Reference No.: _____

SERVICE ANIMALS

Dog Guide Name: _____
Kennel Size: _____
Kennel No.: _____
My Pug Size:
🐾 From the tip of nose to end of tail: _____
🐾 Floor to chest: _____
🐾 Twice the width of the dog shoulder to shoulder: _____
🐾 Floor to top of head for height: _____

TRAIN TRACKER
Pets Friendly Train Journey

Destination: _____   **Number of Days:** _____

Travel Dates: _____   **Number of Nights:** _____

DEPARTURE

Leaving: _____ At: _____
Arriving: _____ At: _____
By: _____
Layovers: _____
Reference No.: _____

ARRIVAL

Leaving: _____ At: _____
Arriving: _____ At: _____
By: _____
Layovers: _____
Reference No.: _____

TRANSPORTATION

Train No.: _____
Pick Up: _____ Drop Off: _____
Company: _____
Contact: _____
Reference No.: _____

SERVICE ANIMALS

Dog Guide Name: _____
Kennel Size: _____
Kennel No.: _____
My Pug Size:
🐾 From the tip of nose to end of tail: _____
🐾 Floor to chest: _____
🐾 Twice the width of the dog shoulder to shoulder: _____
🐾 Floor to top of head for height: _____

87

PLANE TRACKER
Pets Friendly Airlines

Destination: _____   **Number of Days:** _____

Travel Dates: _____   **Number of Nights:** _____

DEPARTURE

Leaving: _____ At: _____
Arriving: _____ At: _____
By: _____
Layovers: _____
Reference No.: _____

ARRIVAL

Leaving: _____ At: _____
Arriving: _____ At: _____
By: _____
Layovers: _____
Reference No.: _____

TRANSPORTATION

Flight No.: _____
Pick Up: _____ Drop Off: _____
Company: _____
Contact: _____
Reference No.: _____

SERVICE ANIMALS

Dog Guide Name: _____
Kennel Size: _____
Kennel No.: _____
My Pug Size:
🐾 From the tip of nose to end of tail: _____
🐾 Floor to chest: _____
🐾 Twice the width of the dog shoulder to shoulder: _____
🐾 Floor to top of head for height: _____

References:

"What Are the Pros and Cons of Owning a Pug?" Quora. Accessed August 3, 2022. https://www.quora.com/What-are-the-pros-and-cons-of-owning-a-pug.

Airpets International. "Flying a Pug," July 25, 2017. https://airpetsinternational.com/flying-a-pug/.

Albert Park Vet. "Brachycephalic Syndrome: A Must Read for All Bulldog and Pug Lovers," October 10, 2017. https://www.albertparkvet.com.au/dog-stuff/2017/10/10/brachycephalic-syndrome-a-must-read-for-all-bulldog-and-pug-lovers.

Balcomb, Brittany. "Travelling With Your Pet - What Are The Real Pros And Cons?" TravelOnline, January 3, 2020. https://www.travelonline.com/news/pros-and-cons-of-travelling-with-your-pet.

Bauhaus, Jean Marie. "All About Brachycephalic Dogs." Hill's Pet Nutrition, May 23, 2018. https://www.hillspet.com/dog-care/behavior-appearance/brachycephalic-dogs.

BePug.com. "Pros and Cons Of Owning a Pug: (Before You Go Out and Get It!)," December 14, 2018. https://bepug.com/pros-and-cons-of-owning-a-pug/.

Blue Cross. "Things to Think about before Buying a Flat-Faced (Brachycephalic) Dog." Accessed August 3, 2022. https://www.bluecross.org.uk/advice/dog/things-to-think-about-before-buying-a-flat-faced-brachycephalic-dog.

Clark, Mike. "Going Boating With Your Dog? Follow These Safety Tips." DogTime, June 28, 2021. https://dogtime.com/how-to/pet-safety/64471-safety-tips-boating-dog.

deBara, Deanna. "Can I Take My Dog to Europe?" The Dog People by Rover.com, July 9, 2019. https://www.rover.com/blog/can-i-take-my-dog-to-europe/.

DogBreeds911.com. "Pug Pros and Cons." Accessed August 3, 2022. https://www.dogbreeds911.com/small-dog-breeds-pug.html.

Elliott, Pippa. "The Problem With Pugs: Brachycephalic Syndrome." Petful, November 7, 2014. https://www.petful.com/pet-health/brachycephalic-syndrome/.

Im, Jimmy. "Should You Travel with Your Pet? The PROS and CONS You Didn't Know." Travelbinger.com, July 8, 2022. https://www.travelbinger.com/pros-and-cons-for-traveling-with-pet/.

Johnston, Chalene. "17 Pros And (Cons) Of Owning A Pug." Dog Breeds FAQ, July 5, 2019. https://dogbreedsfaq.com/asian-dog-breeds/chinese-dog-breeds-list/pug-pros-and-cons/.

Kazimierska, Marika. "Let's Weigh the Pros and Cons of Traveling With a Dog." TheTravel, February 19, 2020. https://www.thetravel.com/traveling-with-dog-pros-and-cons/.

Lowrey, Sassafras. "Brachycephalic Dog Breeds: A Guide to Flat-Faced Dogs." American Kennel Club, October 22, 2021. https://www.akc.org/expert-advice/dog-breeds/brachycephalic-dog-breeds/.

PetRelocation. "Flying With Pugs & Other Snub-Nosed Breeds: 2022 Airline Rules, Restrictions & Alternatives," November 23, 2021. https://www.petrelocation.com/blog/post/flying-with-pugs-other-snub-nosed-breeds-2022.

PetRelocation. "Safety Tips for Flying Internationally with a Pug." Accessed August 3, 2022. https://www.petrelocation.com/blog/post/safety-tips-for-flying-internationally-with-a-pug.

Petsforcare. "Pros and Cons of Owning a Pug," May 21, 2022. https://

petsforcare.com/pros-and-cons-of-owning-a-pug-dog/.

Playforth, Laura. "I've a Flat-Faced Dog Such as a French Bulldog. What Do I Need to Know?" Vets Now, April 20, 2021. https://www.vets-now.com/pet-care-advice/flat-faced-brachycephalic-dogs-need-to-know/.

Polat, Anil. "Traveling with a Pug." GoPetFriendly.com, October 18, 2009. https://www.gopetfriendly.com/blog/traveling-with-a-pug/.

Riana. "The Pros & Cons of Travel with a Dog." Teaspoon of Adventure, August 16, 2019. https://teaspoonofadventure.com/travel-with-a-dog/.

RSPCA Knowledgebase. "What Do I Need to Know about Brachycephalic Dogs?," May 16, 2022. https://kb.rspca.org.au/knowledge-base/what-do-i-need-to-know-about-brachycephalic-dogs/.

The Humane Society Veterinary Medical Association. "The Cost of Cuteness: Health and Welfare Issues Associated with Brachycephalic Dogs." Accessed August 3, 2022. https://www.hsvma.org/brachycephalic.

VIAJEROS PERRUNOS. "Advantages and disadvantages of traveling with a dog," May 5, 2017. https://www.viajerosperrunos.com/single-post/advantages-disadvantages-traveling-with-dog.

Walkin' Pets Blog. "What You Need to Know About Brachycephalic Dogs," November 12, 2021. https://www.handicappedpets.com/blog/what-you-need-to-know-about-brachycephalic-dogs/.

Weir, Malcolm, Krista Williams, and Cheryl Yuill. "Brachycephalic Airway Syndrome in Dogs." VCA Animal Hospital. Accessed August 3, 2022. https://vcahospitals.com/know-your-pet/brachycephalic-airway-syndrome-in-dogs.

Wilber, Jennifer. "The History of Pugs in Ancient China." PetHelpful, April 13, 2022. https://pethelpful.com/dogs/This-History-of-Pugs-in-Ancient-China.

www.ingramcontent.com/pod-product-compliance
Lightning Source LLC
Chambersburg PA
CBHW060346130626
46553CB00003B/1101

* 9 7 9 8 9 8 6 1 6 6 0 2 5 *